Title: Unstoppable Increase: Unlocking the Power of Biblical Principles for Abundance

Introduction:

In a world full of uncertainties and challenges, it's natural to seek stability and security. Many people believe that the only way to achieve this is by accumulating wealth and possessions. While financial prosperity is not necessarily a bad thing, it's important to understand that true abundance goes beyond material possessions. The Bible teaches us that God desires to bless us and increase us in all areas of life.

God has created us to live a life of abundance and increase. From the very beginning, God commanded us to be fruitful and multiply, to fill the earth and subdue it. (Genesis 1:28) This is a promise of increase and prosperity that God has made to each and every one of us.

However, many of us have experienced setbacks and challenges that have made it difficult to live a life of increase. We may have faced financial struggles, health issues, or personal difficulties that have hindered our progress and made it difficult to move forward.

In "Unstoppable Increase," we explore the biblical principles of increase and prosperity, and we learn how we can overcome the obstacles that have held us back. Through scripture and real-life examples, we discover the power of faith, prayer, and obedience, and we learn how these principles can help us to achieve our goals and live a life of abundance.

We will also explore the role of gratitude and generosity in our journey towards increase. We will learn how a heart of gratitude can open doors of opportunity and blessing, and we will discover how our generosity can be a powerful catalyst for increase in our lives and the lives of those around us.

Moreover, we will hear from people who have experienced unstoppable increase in their own lives. We will learn from their stories and gain inspiration from their successes. Through their experiences, we will see that the principles of increase are not just theoretical, but are practical and effective in everyday life.

This book is a call to live a life of increase and abundance, and to embrace the promises that God has made to us. It is a reminder that we serve a God of increase, and that His desire is for us to live a life of prosperity and blessing. We invite you to join us on this journey of faith, and we pray that this book will be a source of inspiration and encouragement as you pursue unstoppable increase in every area of your life.

Chapter 1:

The Source of Increase

The Bible teaches us that God is the source of all increase. In Deuteronomy 8:18, it says, "But remember the Lord your God, for it is he who gives you the ability to produce wealth." When we recognize that our blessings come from God, we can trust that our increase will not be limited by our own abilities or circumstances. In fact, the Bible promises that God will supply all our needs according to his riches in glory (Philippians 4:19).

The source of increase is a fundamental principle that acknowledges that all good things come from God. As believers, we recognize that God is the ultimate source of our blessings and prosperity, and that we are simply stewards of the resources He has given us. Here are a few ways to incorporate the principle of the source of increase into our lives:

Trust in God's provision: We can trust that God will provide for our needs and bless us with abundance when we seek Him first. This means putting our faith in Him and not relying solely on our own efforts or resources.

Seek God's wisdom: As stewards, we can seek God's wisdom to guide our decisions and actions. This includes seeking His guidance in our finances, careers, relationships, and other areas of life.

Honor God with our resources: We can honor God by using our resources wisely and for His purposes. This means using our time, talents, and money in ways that reflect our values and bring glory to Him.

Give generously: A key aspect of the source of increase is giving generously. This includes giving back to God through tithes and offerings, as well as giving to others in need. When we give generously, we acknowledge that all good things come from God, and we trust that He will continue to provide for us.

Scripture is replete with examples of God's desire for us to experience increase and abundance. Here are a few examples:

Giving leads to increase

One of the foundational principles of increase is generosity. When we give of our time, talents, and resources, we open the door for God to bless us in return. Proverbs 11:25 says, "A generous person will prosper; whoever refreshes others will be refreshed."

In the New Testament, we see an example of this in the story of the widow's offering. In Mark 12:41-44, Jesus observes a poor widow giving two small coins in the temple treasury. He tells his disciples that she has given more than all the others, because she gave out of her poverty, while they gave out of their wealth. Jesus is not just commending her sacrificial giving, but also pointing out that her act of generosity will lead to increase in her life.

Obedience leads to increase

Another principle of increase is obedience to God's commands. **Deuteronomy 28:1-2** says, "If you fully obey the Lord your God and carefully follow all his commands I give you today, the Lord your God will set you high above all the nations on earth. All these blessings will come on you and accompany you if you obey the Lord your God."

In the New Testament, we see the story of Peter and the miraculous catch of fish **in Luke 5:1-11.** After a long night of fishing with no success, Jesus tells Peter to cast his net on the other side of the boat. Peter obeys, and they catch so many fish that their nets begin to break. This is not just a story about a miraculous catch of fish, but also a lesson on the power of obedience to God's commands.

Faith leads to increase

Finally, another key principle of increase is faith. **Hebrews 11:6** says, "And without faith it is impossible to please God, because anyone who comes to him must believe that he exists and that he rewards those who earnestly seek him."

In the New Testament, we see the story of the woman with the issue of blood in **Mark 5:25-34**. She had been suffering for years and had tried every medical treatment available, but nothing had worked. However, when she heard about Jesus, she had faith that if she could just touch his cloak, she would be healed. She acted on her faith and was indeed healed. Jesus commended her for her faith, saying, "Daughter, your faith has healed you. Go in peace and be freed from your suffering."

These are just a few examples of the biblical principles of increase. When we give generously, obey God's commands, and have faith in Him, we open the door for God's blessings and provision in our lives.

Chapter 2:

The Principle of Sowing and Reaping

The principle of sowing and reaping is a foundational principle of biblical increase. In Galatians 6:7, it says, "Do not be deceived: God cannot be mocked. A man reaps what he sows." This principle applies to all areas of life, not just finances. If we sow kindness, we will reap kindness. If we sow love, we will reap love. If we sow generosity, we will reap generosity. When we sow into the lives of others, we open ourselves up to receive abundance in return.

This principle teaches us that the choices we make today will have consequences in the future. If we sow seeds of kindness, love, and generosity, we will reap a harvest of blessings in due time. But if we sow seeds of negativity, selfishness, and sin, we will also reap the consequences of our actions.

The principle of sowing and reaping is not just about material possessions, but also about spiritual growth. If we invest in our relationship with God and sow seeds of obedience, prayer, and faith, we will reap a harvest of spiritual blessings and growth.

Here are some scriptural examples of this principle:

Galatians 6:7-8 - "Do not be deceived: God cannot be mocked. A man reaps what he sows. Whoever sows to please their flesh, from the flesh will reap destruction; whoever sows to please the Spirit, from the Spirit will reap eternal life."

This passage is a warning against the deception of thinking that we can sow to the flesh and still reap a harvest of blessing. It emphasizes the importance of sowing to please the Spirit if we want to reap eternal life.

2 Corinthians 9:6 - "Remember this: Whoever sows sparingly will also reap sparingly, and whoever sows generously will also reap generously."

This verse teaches us that the amount we sow will directly impact the amount we reap. If we sow sparingly, we will also reap sparingly, but if we sow generously, we will also reap generously.

Luke 6:38 - "Give, and it will be given to you. A good measure, pressed down, shaken together and running over, will be poured into your lap. For with the measure you use, it will be measured to you."

This verse speaks directly to the principle of sowing and reaping in the context of giving. It tells us that when we give generously, we will also receive generously.

Proverbs 11:24-25 - "One person gives freely, yet gains even more; another withholds unduly, but comes to poverty. A generous person will prosper; whoever refreshes others will be refreshed."

This passage teaches us that when we give freely and generously, we will actually gain more in return. It emphasizes the importance of sowing into the lives of others and refreshing them, which will ultimately result in our own increase.

Another important point to consider regarding the principle of sowing and reaping is that the harvest may not always be immediate or visible. Sometimes we may not see the results of our sowing until much later, or in unexpected ways. This requires patience, faith, and trust in God's timing and purposes.

Furthermore, the quality and quantity of our harvest will depend on the quality and quantity of our sowing. Just as a farmer must carefully prepare the soil and plant the seeds in order to reap a bountiful harvest, we must also invest time, effort, and resources into the things that we want to see grow and flourish in our lives.

Finally, it's important to note that the principle of sowing and reaping is not a magic formula for success or a guarantee of prosperity. It's not simply a matter of doing good things so that good things will happen to us. Rather, it's a reflection of the natural laws that God has established in the world, and a call to align our actions and attitudes with His will and purposes.

In summary, the principle of sowing and reaping is a powerful reminder that our actions have consequences, both in this life and the next. By sowing seeds of faith, love, and service, we can reap a harvest of blessings and abundance that will far outweigh any temporary setbacks or challenges we may face along the way.

When we understand this principle and apply it in our lives, we can experience the blessings of increase and abundance that God desires for us.

Chapter 3:

The Principle of Faith

The principle of faith is another essential principle of biblical increase. Hebrews 11:6 says, "And without faith, it is impossible to please God, because anyone who comes to him must believe that he exists and that he rewards those who earnestly seek him." When we have faith in God's promises, we position ourselves to receive his blessings. This faith must be accompanied by action, as James 2:26 says, "Faith without works is dead." When we step out in faith and act on God's promises, we position ourselves for increase.

The Bible teaches that faith is the substance of things hoped for and the evidence of things not seen (Hebrews 11:1).

The principle of faith is a fundamental biblical concept that is central to the Christian life. Faith is often defined as a belief or trust in something or someone, particularly in God and His promises.

Faith is the foundation upon which we build our relationship with God. It is by faith that we accept His grace and salvation, and it is through faith that we can access His power and blessings. Jesus Himself emphasized the importance of faith. The principle of faith also has implications for our daily lives. It requires us to trust in God's goodness and provision, even when circumstances may seem difficult or uncertain. It calls us to step out in obedience and take risks, knowing that God is faithful to fulfill His promises. It enables us to overcome fear and doubt, and to persevere in the face of adversity.

Moreover, faith is not just a passive belief or intellectual assent, but an active, living relationship with God. James 2:17-18 says, "Thus also faith by itself, if it does not have works, is dead. But someone will say, 'You have faith, and I have works.' Show me your faith without your works, and I will show you my faith by my works." In other words, true faith is evidenced by our actions and obedience to God's will.

In summary, the principle of faith is a foundational aspect of the Christian life. It requires us to trust in God's promises, step out in obedience, and live out our faith through our actions. By cultivating a strong and active faith, we can experience the fullness of God's blessings and power in our lives.

Here are some scriptural examples of this principle:

Mark 11:22-24 - "Have faith in God," Jesus answered. "Truly I tell you, if anyone says to this mountain, 'Go, throw yourself into the sea,' and does not doubt in their heart but believes that what they say will happen, it will be done for them. Therefore I tell you, whatever you ask for in prayer, believe that you have received it, and it will be yours."

This passage teaches us that faith is a powerful force that can move mountains. It emphasizes the importance of believing that what we ask for in prayer will be done for us.

Matthew 17:20 - "Because you have so little faith. Truly I tell you, if you have faith as small as a mustard seed, you can say to this mountain, 'Move from here to there,' and it will move. Nothing will be impossible for you."

This verse tells us that even a small amount of faith can have a powerful impact. It emphasizes the importance of having faith, even when our circumstances seem impossible.

Hebrews 11:6 - "And without faith it is impossible to please God, because anyone who comes to him must believe that he exists and that he rewards those who earnestly seek him."

This verse teaches us that faith is necessary to please God. It emphasizes the importance of believing in God and trusting that He will reward those who seek Him.

James 1:6 - "But when you ask, you must believe and not doubt, because the one who doubts is like a wave of the sea, blown and tossed by the wind."

This verse teaches us that doubt can undermine our faith and prevent us from receiving the blessings that God has for us. It emphasizes the importance of believing and not doubting when we ask God for something.

When we exercise faith in God and His promises, we position ourselves for increase and abundance.

Chapter 4:

The Principle of Stewardship

The principle of stewardship teaches us to be faithful with what God has entrusted to us. In Luke 16:10, it says, "Whoever can be trusted with very little can also be trusted with much, and whoever is dishonest with very little will also be dishonest with much." When we are faithful with the resources God has given us, we position ourselves to receive even more. This principle applies not only to finances but to all areas of life.

Stewardship is another important principle that is essential for increase. This principle teaches us that we are not owners but rather stewards of everything that God has given us.

Stewardship is about managing and taking care of the resources and blessings that have been entrusted to us. This includes everything from our time and talents to our money and possessions. As stewards, we recognize that everything we have comes from God, and we are responsible for using these resources wisely and for His purposes. Here are a few ways to incorporate the principle of stewardship into our lives:

Cultivate gratitude: Stewardship begins with recognizing the blessings in our lives and being grateful for them. By cultivating a sense of gratitude, we can begin to view our resources as gifts to be shared and used for the greater good.

Use resources wisely: Being a good steward means using our resources wisely and responsibly. This could mean creating a budget to manage our finances, using our time efficiently, or taking care of the environment by conserving resources.

Share with others: A key aspect of stewardship is sharing our blessings with others. This can take many forms, from donating to charity to volunteering our time and talents to help those in need.

Invest in the future: Good stewards recognize the importance of investing in the future. This could mean saving for retirement, investing in education or training, or supporting initiatives that promote sustainability and long-term well-being.

Here are some scriptural examples of this principle:

Matthew 25:14-30 - The Parable of the Talents is a powerful illustration of the principle of stewardship. In this parable, a master entrusts his servants with different amounts of money, and he expects them to use the money wisely and increase it. The servants who are faithful with what they have been given are rewarded with even more, while the one who is unfaithful is punished.

This parable emphasizes the importance of stewarding what God has given us and using it wisely to produce increase.

1 Peter 4:10 - "Each of you should use whatever gift you have received to serve others, as faithful stewards of God's grace in its various forms."

This verse teaches us that we have all been given gifts and talents by God, and we are called to use them to serve others as faithful stewards of God's grace. It emphasizes the importance of using our talents and resources to bless others and further God's kingdom.

Luke 16:10-12 - "Whoever can be trusted with very little can also be trusted with much, and whoever is dishonest with very little will also be dishonest with much. So if you have not been trustworthy in handling worldly wealth, who will trust you with true riches? And if you have not been trustworthy with someone else's property, who will give you property of your own?"

This passage emphasizes the importance of being faithful with the resources and opportunities that God has given us. It emphasizes the idea that if we are faithful in small things, God will entrust us with even greater things.

1 Corinthians 4:2 - "Now it is required that those who have been given a trust must prove faithful."

This verse teaches us that stewardship is a responsibility and requires faithfulness. It emphasizes the importance of being faithful with what we have been entrusted with.

When we understand and apply this principle in our lives, we can experience the blessings of increase and abundance that come from being faithful stewards of what God has given us.

Chapter 5:

The Principle of Generosity

The principle of generosity is a powerful principle of biblical increase. In 2 Corinthians 9:6-7, it says, "Remember this: Whoever sows sparingly will also reap sparingly, and whoever sows generously will also reap generously. Each of you should give what you have decided in your heart to give, not reluctantly or under compulsion, for God loves a cheerful giver." When we give generously, we open ourselves up to receive generously in return. Generosity is not only about finances but about our time, talents, and resources.

This principle teaches us that giving generously is a key to experiencing increase in our lives.

The principle of generosity is about giving freely and generously, without expectation of anything in return. This can take many forms, from donating money or time to charitable causes, to showing kindness and compassion to others in our daily interactions.

Give freely: Giving generously doesn't necessarily mean giving a lot. It's about giving freely, without reservation or expectation of anything in return. This can be as simple as offering a compliment or a kind word to someone who needs it.

Give regularly: Cultivating a habit of giving can help us stay focused on the needs of others and make giving a natural part of our lives. Whether it's a regular donation to a favorite charity or volunteering at a local food bank, making giving a regular part of our routine can help us stay connected to the principle of generosity.

Give sacrificially: Sometimes, giving generously means making a sacrifice in our own lives. This could mean donating money we might have otherwise spent on ourselves, or giving up our time to help someone in need. By giving sacrificially, we can cultivate a deeper sense of compassion and empathy for others.

Give with love: The principle of generosity is ultimately about showing love and compassion to others. By giving with love, we can create a ripple effect of positivity and kindness in the world.

Here are some scriptural examples of this principle:

Luke 6:38 - "Give, and it will be given to you. A good measure, pressed down, shaken together and running over, will be poured into your lap. For with the measure you use, it will be measured to you."

This verse emphasizes the importance of giving generously. It teaches us that when we give generously, we will receive generously. The measure that we use in giving is the same measure that will be used in giving back to us.

Proverbs 11:24-25 - "One person gives freely, yet gains even more; another withholds unduly, but comes to poverty. A generous person will prosper; whoever refreshes others will be refreshed."

This passage emphasizes the importance of generosity in experiencing increase. It teaches us that when we give freely, we will gain even more. Those who are generous will prosper, while those who withhold will come to poverty.

2 Corinthians 9:6-8 - "Remember this: Whoever sows sparingly will also reap sparingly, and whoever sows generously will also reap generously. Each of you should give what you have decided in your heart to give, not reluctantly or under compulsion, for God loves a cheerful giver. And God is able to bless you abundantly, so that in all things at all times, having all that you need, you will abound in every good work."

This passage emphasizes the importance of giving generously and cheerfully. It teaches us that when we give generously, we will reap generously. God is able to bless us abundantly so that we will have all that we need and abound in every good work.

Malachi 3:10 - "Bring the whole tithe into the storehouse, that there may be food in my house. Test me in this," says the Lord Almighty, "and see if I will not throw open the floodgates of heaven and pour out so much blessing that there will not be room enough to store it."

This verse emphasizes the importance of tithing and giving to the work of God. It teaches us that when we give to God, He will pour out blessings on us that we cannot even contain.

When we understand and apply this principle in our lives, we can experience the blessings of increase and abundance that come from giving generously.

Feeding of the 5,000 in John 6:1-15 also teaches us about the importance of sharing and generosity. When the boy who had the five loaves and two fish offered them to Jesus, he did not hold back or worry about what he would eat later. Instead, he gave everything he had to Jesus, who used it to feed the entire crowd.

This reminds us that we should not be selfish with what we have been given, but rather should be willing to share and give to those in need. When we are generous and give freely, God can use our gifts to bless others in ways we never thought possible.

Chapter 6:

The Principle of Gratitude

The principle of gratitude teaches us to be thankful for what God has given us. In 1 Thessalonians 5:18, it says, "Give thanks in all circumstances; for this is God's will for you in Christ Jesus."This principle teaches us the importance of being grateful for what we have and focusing on the blessings in our lives.

The principle of gratitude is a powerful tool for cultivating a mindset of abundance and attracting more positive experiences into our lives. It involves focusing on the good things in our lives, rather than dwelling on what we lack or what's going wrong.

Gratitude journaling: Taking time each day to write down a few things we're grateful for can help us cultivate a more positive mindset. This can be as simple as jotting down a few bullet points each morning or evening.

Gratitude affirmations: Affirmations are positive statements we repeat to ourselves to reinforce a desired mindset or belief. Incorporating gratitude affirmations into our daily routine can help us stay focused on the good things in our lives.

Gratitude in relationships: Expressing gratitude to the people in our lives can strengthen our relationships and create a positive feedback loop. By acknowledging and appreciating the good things others do for us, we encourage them to continue those behaviors.

Gratitude in adversity: Even in challenging times, there are often things we can be grateful for. By focusing on the positive aspects of a difficult situation, we can cultivate resilience and a sense of empowerment.

Gratitude as a lifestyle: Ultimately, the principle of gratitude is about cultivating a mindset of abundance and joy. By making gratitude a daily habit, we can create a more positive and fulfilling life.

Here are some scriptural examples of this principle:

Psalm 100:4 - "Enter his gates with thanksgiving and his courts with praise; give thanks to him and praise his name."

This verse teaches us that we should approach God with thanksgiving and praise. By focusing on the blessings in our lives and expressing gratitude to God, we can cultivate a spirit of thankfulness that can lead to increase.

Philippians 4:6-7 - "Do not be anxious about anything, but in every situation, by prayer and petition, with thanksgiving, present your requests to God. And the peace of God, which transcends all understanding, will guard your hearts and your minds in Christ Jesus."

This passage emphasizes the importance of prayer and thanksgiving. By bringing our requests to God with thanksgiving, we can experience the peace of God and guard our hearts and minds from anxiety and worry.

Colossians 3:15-17 - "Let the peace of Christ rule in your hearts, since as members of one body you were called to peace. And be thankful. Let the message of Christ dwell among you richly as you teach and admonish one another with all wisdom through psalms, hymns, and songs from the Spirit, singing to God with gratitude in your hearts. And whatever you do, whether in word or deed, do it all in the name of the Lord Jesus, giving thanks to God the Father through him."

This passage emphasizes the importance of gratitude and thankfulness in our daily lives. We should let the peace of Christ rule in our hearts and be thankful in all circumstances. By singing and giving thanks to God, we can cultivate a spirit of gratitude that can lead to increase in our lives.

Luke 17:11-19 - This passage tells the story of ten lepers who were healed by Jesus, but only one returned to give thanks. Jesus praised the one who returned and said, "Rise and go; your faith has made you well."

This story emphasizes the importance of giving thanks and expressing gratitude. By being thankful for what we have, we can experience healing and increase in our lives.

By focusing on the blessings in our lives and expressing gratitude to God, we can cultivate a spirit of thankfulness that can lead to increase and abundance.

Chapter 7:

Living a Life of Unstoppable Increase

Living a life of unstoppable increase requires a combination of principles and actions, as well as a mindset of faith and perseverance.

Living a life of unstoppable increase involves taking intentional actions to cultivate growth and abundance in all areas of our lives.

Gratitude: Gratitude is a powerful practice that can help us focus on what we have rather than what we lack. By cultivating gratitude, we can shift our mindset towards abundance and attract more positive experiences into our lives. One way to practice gratitude is to keep a gratitude journal and write down three things we're grateful for each day.

Continuous learning: To experience unstoppable increase, it's important to continuously learn and grow. This can involve reading books, taking courses, attending workshops, or seeking out mentors who can guide us on our journey. By expanding our knowledge and skills, we can open up new opportunities and experiences in our lives.

Taking action: Without action, even the best intentions and ideas are just dreams. To live a life of unstoppable increase, it's important to take intentional action towards our goals and aspirations. This can involve setting clear goals, breaking them down into smaller steps, and taking consistent action towards them.

Generosity: Generosity involves giving freely of our time, resources, and talents to others. By practicing generosity, we can cultivate a mindset of abundance and attract more positivity into our lives. This can involve volunteering in our community, donating to charitable causes, or simply being kind and helpful to those around us.

Self-care: Taking care of ourselves is essential for experiencing unstoppable increase in all areas of our lives. This can involve prioritizing our physical health, mental wellbeing, and spiritual practices. By investing in ourselves, we can show up as our best selves and create a positive ripple effect in the world around us.

By incorporating these practices into our daily lives, we can live a life of unstoppable increase and experience growth, abundance, and fulfillment in all areas of our lives.

Here are some scriptural examples of how we can live a life of unstoppable increase:

Proverbs 3:5-6 - "Trust in the Lord with all your heart and lean not on your own understanding; in all your ways submit to him, and he will make your paths straight."

This verse emphasizes the importance of trust in God and submission to His will. By putting our faith in Him and following His guidance, we can experience a life of increase and success.

Joshua 1:8 - "Keep this Book of the Law always on your lips; meditate on it day and night, so that you may be careful to do everything written in it. Then you will be prosperous and successful."

This verse emphasizes the importance of studying and meditating on the Word of God. By aligning our thoughts and actions with His teachings, we can experience prosperity and success.

Luke 6:38 - "Give, and it will be given to you. A good measure, pressed down, shaken together and running over, will be poured into your lap. For with the measure you use, it will be measured to you."

This verse emphasizes the principle of generosity and giving. By giving generously to others, we can experience increase in our own lives.

2 Corinthians 9:6-8 - "Remember this: Whoever sows sparingly will also reap sparingly, and whoever sows generously will also reap generously. Each of you should give what you have decided in your heart to give, not reluctantly or under compulsion, for God loves a cheerful giver. And God is able to bless you abundantly, so that in all things at all times, having all that you need, you will abound in every good work."

This passage emphasizes the principle of sowing and reaping. By sowing generously **and cheerfully, we can experience abundance and increase in our lives.**

Philippians 4:13 - "I can do all this through him who gives me strength."

This verse emphasizes the importance of faith and perseverance. By putting our trust in God and relying on His strength, we can overcome obstacles and experience unstoppable increase in our lives.

By following these principles and putting our faith in God, we can experience abundance, prosperity, and success in all areas of our lives.

Chapter 8:

Overcoming Obstacles to Unstoppable Increase

Obstacles are a natural part of life and can often hinder our pursuit of unstoppable increase. However, the Bible offers guidance and encouragement on how to overcome these obstacles and experience continued growth and success.

Fear: Fear can hold us back from taking risks and pursuing new opportunities. However, it's important to remember that fear is often based on irrational or exaggerated beliefs. One way to overcome fear is to challenge these beliefs and replace them with more positive and empowering ones. For example, instead of believing that failure is inevitable, we can focus on the potential rewards and lessons learned from taking action.

Lack of clarity: Without a clear vision and plan for our lives, it's easy to feel lost and overwhelmed. To overcome this obstacle, it's important to take time to reflect on our goals and priorities, and to break them down into smaller, achievable steps. By focusing on one step at a time, we can gradually build momentum and make progress towards our desired outcome.

Self-doubt: Negative self-talk and self-doubt can undermine our confidence and prevent us from taking action. To overcome this obstacle, it's important to practice self-compassion and to focus on our strengths and achievements. Surrounding ourselves with supportive and encouraging people can also help us build our confidence and belief in ourselves.

Limited resources: Financial, time, and other resources can be a major obstacle to experiencing unstoppable increase. However, it's important to remember that resourcefulness is often more important than resources themselves. By being creative and resourceful, we can often find ways to overcome limitations and achieve our goals. For example, we can leverage technology to save time and automate certain tasks, or we can collaborate with others to pool our resources and skills.

By recognizing and addressing these obstacles, we can overcome them and experience the fullness of unstoppable increase in our lives.

Here are some scriptural examples of how we can overcome obstacles to unstoppable increase:

Philippians 4:6-7 - "Do not be anxious about anything, but in every situation, by prayer and petition, with thanksgiving, present your requests to God. And the peace of God, which transcends all understanding, will guard your hearts and your minds in Christ Jesus."

This verse emphasizes the importance of prayer and giving our anxieties to God. By turning to Him in times of trouble, we can experience peace and overcome obstacles that may be hindering our progress.

Isaiah 41:10 - "So do not fear, for I am with you; do not be dismayed, for I am your God. I will strengthen you and help you; I will uphold you with my righteous right hand."

This verse emphasizes the importance of trusting in God and relying on His strength. By placing our faith in Him, we can overcome fear and doubt that may be preventing us from achieving unstoppable increase.

James 1:2-4 - "Consider it pure joy, my brothers and sisters, whenever you face trials of many kinds, because you know that the testing of your faith produces perseverance. Let perseverance finish its work so that you may be mature and complete, not lacking anything."

This passage emphasizes the importance of perseverance and viewing obstacles as opportunities for growth. By staying committed to our goals and trusting in God's plan, we can overcome challenges and experience unstoppable increase.

Philippians 3:13-14 - "Brothers and sisters, I do not consider myself yet to have taken hold of it. But one thing I do: Forgetting what is behind and straining toward what is ahead, I press on toward the goal to win the prize for which God has called me heavenward in Christ Jesus."

This verse emphasizes the importance of focusing on the future and not dwelling on past failures or setbacks. By maintaining a forward-looking mindset, we can overcome obstacles and achieve unstoppable increase.

Romans 8:28 - "And we know that in all things God works for the good of those who love him, who have been called according to his purpose."

This verse emphasizes the belief that God can turn even the most difficult situations into blessings. By trusting in His plan and purpose, we can overcome obstacles and experience unstoppable increase.

By following these principles and trusting in God, we can persevere through challenges and achieve success in all areas of our lives.

UNTOPPABLE INCREASE HAS ACT OF ABUNDACE

The principle of unstoppable increase involves an attitude of abundance, which is rooted in the belief that God is a generous provider who desires to bless His people. This attitude is based on the biblical concept of abundance, which is the idea that God's blessings are not limited, but rather are abundant and overflowing.

An attitude of abundance involves trusting in God's provision, even in times of scarcity or difficulty. It means recognizing that God's resources are not limited and that He is able to provide for all our needs. This attitude also involves being generous with what we have, recognizing that we have been blessed in order to be a blessing to others.

Jesus spoke about this attitude of abundance in John 10:10, where He said, "The thief does not come except to steal, and to kill, and to destroy. I have come that they may have life, and that they may have it more abundantly." In other words, Jesus came to give us a life that is full and overflowing, not just in material blessings, but in spiritual and emotional abundance as well.

The principle of unstoppable increase, then, is not just about accumulating wealth or success, but about living a life of abundance and generosity. As we trust in God's provision and seek to bless others, we will experience a sense of joy and fulfillment that cannot be found in material possessions alone.

Yes, the principle of abundance and generosity is rooted in several scriptures in the Bible. Here are a few examples:

Luke 6:38 - "Give, and it will be given to you. A good measure, pressed down, shaken together and running over, will be poured into your lap. For with the measure you use, it will be measured to you."

This scripture emphasizes the principle of sowing and reaping, which is closely related to the principle of abundance. When we give generously, we can expect to receive generously in return.

Proverbs 11:25 - "A generous person will prosper; whoever refreshes others will be refreshed."

This scripture emphasizes the idea that generosity leads to abundance. When we bless others, we are blessed in return.

2 Corinthians 9:6-8 - "Remember this: Whoever sows sparingly will also reap sparingly, and whoever sows generously will also reap generously. Each of you should give what you have decided in your heart to give, not reluctantly or under compulsion, for God loves a cheerful giver. And God is able to bless you abundantly, so that in all things at all times, having all that you need, you will abound in every good work."

This passage highlights the principle of sowing and reaping, as well as the importance of giving cheerfully and generously. It also emphasizes that God is able to bless us abundantly, providing for all our needs so that we can continue to bless others.

Overall, these scriptures and others like them teach us that abundance and generosity are central to the principle of unstoppable increase. By cultivating an attitude of abundance and seeking to bless others, we can experience the fullness of God's blessings and live a life of unstoppable increase.

Abundance and generosity are not just about material wealth, but also include spiritual and emotional blessings. When we give of ourselves, our time, and our resources, we not only bless others but also experience personal growth and fulfillment.

The principle of abundance and generosity requires a mindset shift from scarcity to abundance. We need to trust that God's resources are limitless and that He will provide for all our needs, which allows us to give freely and generously.

Abundance and generosity are not just one-time actions, but are ongoing practices that require consistent effort and commitment. By making generosity a habit, we can experience continuous blessings and increase in all areas of our lives.

When we live a life of abundance and generosity, we create a positive ripple effect in the world around us. Our actions inspire others to give and bless others, creating a culture of generosity and abundance.

UNTOPPABLE INCREASE

The Widow of Zarephath Example

The story of the Widow of Zarephath is found in the Old Testament, in the book of 1 Kings, chapter 17. The story illustrates the concept of unstoppable increase, which means that God's provision can continue to multiply and increase in our lives, even when circumstances seem to indicate the opposite.

The Widow of Zarephath was a poor widow who was gathering sticks to make a fire so that she could prepare a meal for herself and her son. Elijah, a prophet of God, approached her and asked her for some water and bread. The widow replied that she only had a handful of flour and a little oil, and that she was preparing to make a final meal for herself and her son, after which they would die of starvation.

Elijah told the widow to make him a small cake of bread first, and then to make some for herself and her son. He promised her that if she did this, the flour and oil would not run out until the day that God sent rain on the land. The widow obeyed Elijah's instructions, and to her amazement, the flour and oil did not run out. She was able to make enough food for herself, her son, and Elijah, and the provision continued to multiply.

The story of the Widow of Zarephath illustrates the principle of unstoppable increase, which means that when we put our faith and trust in God, He can provide for us in miraculous ways. Despite the fact that the widow had only a small amount of flour and oil, God was able to multiply it to meet her needs and provide for her in abundance.

This story encourages us to trust in God's provision, even when circumstances seem dire and we cannot see a way out. It reminds us that God can take our small offerings and turn them into something great, and that His provision is limitless and unstoppable.

Another important lesson we can learn from the story of the widow of Zarephath is the concept of generosity. Even though the widow had very little, she was willing to share what little she had with Elijah, a stranger who was in need. Her act of generosity and hospitality towards Elijah opened up the door for a miracle in her life. This teaches us that when we are willing to give out of our own need, God can work in our lives in incredible ways.

Moreover, the story of the widow of Zarephath also demonstrates the power of faith. Despite the seemingly impossible situation she was in, the widow chose to trust God's promise through Elijah. She had faith that her jar of flour and jug of oil would not run out, and her faith was rewarded with a miracle. This teaches us that even when we face difficult and trying circumstances, we can choose to have faith and trust in God's promises.

Overall, the story of the widow of Zarephath teaches us important lessons about God's provision, obedience, trust, generosity, and faith. It serves as a powerful reminder that no matter how impossible our situations may seem, God is able to provide for our needs and work miracles in our lives when we trust in Him.

One of the most well-known examples is the story of the multiplication of the loaves and fishes, found in all four Gospels (Matthew 14:13-21, Mark 6:30-44, Luke 9:10-17, and John 6:1-15).

Jesus was preaching to a large crowd of people in a remote area, and the people were becoming hungry. When the disciples found only five loaves of bread and two fish among them, they were concerned about how to feed the thousands of people who had gathered. But Jesus took the bread and fish, gave thanks to God, and began breaking them into pieces. Miraculously, the food multiplied, and everyone was able to eat their fill, with twelve baskets of leftover bread and fish collected at the end.

This is a powerful example of how God can take our meager resources and use them to bring about unstoppable increase. It shows us that when we bring what we have to God, He can work miracles in our lives and provide for our needs in ways that we could never imagine. It also demonstrates the importance of faith and trust in God's power and provision, even in the midst of seemingly impossible situations.

Yes, another example of unstoppable increase is widow's oil, found in **2 Kings 4:1-7.**

In this account, a widow of one of the sons of the prophets approached the prophet Elisha for help. Her husband had died, leaving her with debts she was unable to pay. The creditor was threatening to take her two sons as slaves if she did not pay him back. Elisha asked the widow what she had in her house, and all she had was a small jar of oil.

Elisha instructed the widow to borrow as many empty jars as she could from her neighbors and pour the oil into them. Miraculously, the oil continued to pour out of the small jar and fill up all the borrowed jars until there were no more left. Elisha then instructed the widow to sell the oil and pay off her debts, and she and her sons were able to live on the rest of the proceeds.

God can take our limited resources and bring about unstoppable increase. It shows us that when we are obedient to God's instructions, He can work miracles in our lives and provide for our needs in ways that we could never imagine. It also demonstrates the importance of having faith in God's ability to provide for us, even in the midst of difficult circumstances.

Conclusion

Unstoppable increase is a concept that is rooted in biblical principles of growth and prosperity. By applying the principles of stewardship, sowing and reaping, faith, generosity, gratitude, and more, we can experience unstoppable increase in every area of our lives, including our finances, relationships, and personal development.

It is the idea that God can take our limited resources and use them to bring about miraculous increase and abundance, even in the midst of difficult circumstances.

We have explored and have seen how God can take a little and make it much, how He can bring about miracles when we trust in Him and obey His instructions, and how He can use our generosity and willingness to share to bless others and bring about unstoppable increase in our lives.

Another important theme in the book is the role of faith in experiencing unstoppable increase. We can see that all the main characters had faith in God and trusted in His ability to provide for their needs and work miracles in their lives. Whether it was the widow of Zarephath, the woman with the issue of blood, or the boy with the loaves and fishes, each one had faith in God's power to bring about unstoppable increase.

This is a reminder to us that when we have faith in God, we open ourselves up to experiencing His blessings and provision in our lives. It is through faith that we can see the impossible become possible and experience the unstoppable increase that God has in store for us.

Another important point is the were obedient to God's instructions, even when they didn't make sense or seemed impossible. It was through their obedience that they were able to experience the unstoppable increase that God had in store for them.

When we are obedient to God's instructions, we open ourselves up to experiencing His blessings and provision in our lives. It is through our obedience that God can work miracles in our lives and bring about the unstoppable increase that He has in store for us.

Ultimately, the message of the book is that we can trust in God's provision and His ability to work miracles in our lives. When we have faith in Him and are willing to obey His instructions, we can experience a level of abundance and increase that is truly unstoppable. Whether we are facing financial difficulties, health challenges, or other obstacles, we can look to these stories as examples of how God can take our situation and turn it around for our good.

However, it is important to acknowledge that obstacles and challenges are a natural part of life, and can often hinder our pursuit of unstoppable increase. But as we have seen through the examples of scripture, with prayer, perseverance, and trust in God, we can overcome these obstacles and continue to experience growth and success.

Ultimately, the pursuit of unstoppable increase is not solely about material gain or success, but rather about living a life that is in alignment with God's will and purpose. By prioritizing our relationship with Him and using our blessings to serve others, we can experience a sense of fulfillment and purpose that far exceeds any material gain.

So let us continue to apply these principles of unstoppable increase in our daily lives, trusting in God and His plan for our future. May we be blessed with abundance and prosperity, and may we use our blessings to bless others and make a positive impact on the world around us.

www.ingramcontent.com/pod-product-compliance
Lightning Source LLC
Chambersburg PA
CBHW071126220526
45467CB00004B/2073